# NOT JUST A STATISTIC

## Writings on Life and Baby Loss

**BY ANGELA MARSHALL**

"There are those who sprout
their roots and grow.
There are those who
spread their wings and fly"

In memory of babies due 16th July 2008.
29th May 2017 and 1st February 2018.

Illustration by Joanne Chard @joanneamandadesigns

## Acknowledgements

Cover illustration by: Joanne Chard @joanneamandadesigns
All Poetry Copyright
©Angela Marshall (@angela_writes_life_and_loss)
Year of Publication: 2021
ISBN: 978-1-7399743-0-5

Book Design: Rachel Dickens @lollysnow

Illustrations by:
Page 3 & 63: Joanne Chard @joanneamandadesigns
Page 29: Emma Delgado @Idas_inkling
Page 33, 43 & 133: Stacey Williamson-Michie @awesomemamaillustration
Page 37: Shivani Vij @vesture_voyage
Page 51: Sophie Cook @doodley.bobz
Page 77: Lottie Bolster @lottie_bolster
Page 83: Bethany Field @bethany_field_art
Page 91, 93 & 95: Rachel Dickens @lollysnow
Page 101: Amanda Clarke @amandaclarke_illustration
Back Cover: Alice Atkinson @alice_atkinson_illustration

**A special thanks to 4Louis for their contribution to the final product.**
A minimum of 25% of the profits from each book will be donated to the charity.

In Memory

of

WILL MORAN x xx

# CONTENTS

# Introduction – My Story

# MY STORY

I have grown up knowing about miscarriage and stillbirth, having had family members lose babies at various stages of pregnancy and just after birth. Just prior to my first pregnancy, a friend of a friend suffered their second full term loss. Yet, despite this, I didn't realise how common pregnancy loss was. I also didn't think it would be something that could happen to me.

My husband and I got married in July 2007, and immediately started trying for a baby. We were lucky in that we got pregnant quite quickly. At that time, one of my sisters had just had her first baby and another was also pregnant. It seemed to be good timing that we would all have our babies within nine months of each other.

At first, everything seemed to be going to plan, but when I was around seven weeks pregnant, I had a bleed at work. I was taken to A&E, and my husband was called from work to meet me there. At that point, I didn't really consider miscarriage as a possibility. There was nothing that the hospital could do just then, so I was sent home and asked to come back on the Friday for a scan.

Naturally, I was anxious about the scan, especially when they couldn't see anything abdominally, but an internal scan showed a baby, complete with a heartbeat, approximately seven weeks old, judging by the measurements, which was just as it should have been. I remember going home and showing my parents and my sisters the scan picture, and being so excited as the baby was due on our first wedding anniversary. I was also confident that we had seen a heartbeat, as I had been reassured that the chances of a healthy pregnancy improve after a heartbeat is detected.

Over the coming weeks, I continued to have morning sickness, and I looked and felt pregnant. Due to a delay with the GP, I didn't have my booking in appointment with the midwife until I was eleven weeks pregnant, on Christmas Eve, and my dating scan was booked for fifteen weeks rather than twelve weeks.

In the January, when I was coming up to thirteen weeks pregnant, I had a little bit of brown spotting, and some cramping. I called 111, who advised that it was potentially a miscarriage, and that I should call my GP the next day. I got a scan booked in for the Wednesday, but I think in my heart of hearts I knew at this point that we had lost the baby. Despite this, on the morning before the scan, I told the lady at the bank that I was pregnant and we were going in for a scan. She was the last person I got to tell.

At the hospital, there wasn't a separate space for the early pregnancy unit, so I sat with all of the other expectant parents, and watched as they came out happy and glowing. When we were called through, it was the same as before. An abdominal scan didn't reveal anything, and this confirmed it for me. I should have been 13 weeks pregnant at that point. The baby should have been visible. My husband didn't realise the significance of this, and he was still hopeful as I am emptied my bladder and came back for the internal scan.

Lying there, the silence was deafening as the sonographer turned to us both and said those dreadful words: "I'm sorry – there's no heartbeat." The baby had died at seven weeks and three days, three days after my last scan, six weeks previously. A doctor ran through the options with us, but I knew I wanted surgery, an ERPC (evacuation of retained products of conception). I just wanted the baby out of me. It haunted me to know that I had carried around a dead baby inside of me for all of that time.

We left by the same entrance we had come in, past all the happy, smiling people. I was conscious not to cry too much because I didn't want to upset those people, those strangers, even though inside, my heart was breaking.

My surgery was scheduled for the Friday, and that has to be one of the loneliest experiences of my life. I was admitted on to a general surgical ward, and my husband wasn't allowed past the reception desk. There was limited compassion and understanding and I cried, on my own, until it was time to be taken down to theatre, where I cried as they put me to sleep.

I left hospital that day with a teddy bear my husband had bought me and a sicknote for three days. That was all my baby was worth – three days off sick. In the end, I took two weeks off and I was at least met with care and compassion when I came back to work.

I saw a counsellor at the hospital, but I don't think I took in what she was saying, nor did I like her style, but it didn't matter, as within a few months I was pregnant again. I was determined that this pregnancy would be perfect, it would go to plan and I would have a happy, healthy baby at the end of it. I deserved it. But this pregnancy was fraught with anxiety, from early bleeds and early scans to a complicated birth and delivery. Yes, I had a healthy daughter in 2009, but my expectations of pregnancy and birth left me with a debilitating post-natal depression that I hadn't counted on.

Due to this, it took a long time to decide to try for another baby, and a long time to conceive her. I had the same anxiety-ridden pregnancy, and another complicated birth, this time one in which both myself and the baby could have died, but my second daughter was born healthy in 2013. My husband and I were both reassured that we could have another baby, and, to avoid complications, they would be delivered at 37 weeks.

When we started to try for our third baby, I was aware of the risks of pregnancy and birth, and I was acutely aware of miscarriage, but I had had two healthy children, so we would be fine with a third. In 2016, I fell pregnant for the fourth time, but something felt different, something I couldn't put my finger on. Like my previous pregnancies, I had an early bleed and went to the hospital for an early scan. Although this was a different hospital, and eight years on from my first loss, they didn't have a separate early pregnancy unit either, so again I was forced to sit and wait with the couples waiting for their 12-week scans.

Again, I was told that they couldn't see what they needed to with an abdominal scan and was required to have an internal scan. This time, there was ambiguity. There was a baby, and there was a foetal pole, but it wasn't enough to say that everything was going to be ok. There were questions over how far along I was, with the scan dates being different to what I thought they should have been. I was told that I would need to come back in two weeks to see how things were progressing.

I am not sure if I knew at this point how things were going to end, but I never made it to the second scan. A week later, on a Friday night, I woke up to a massive bleed and my husband rushed me to A&E. I was in agony and nearly collapsing from the blood loss. After I was examined, it was determined that my cervix was still closed, but due to the pain that I was in, they would admit me. They also managed to squeeze in an ultrasound, and there was the baby, with a heartbeat.

On the ward, the doctor came to see me while I was on my own, and told me that due to the amount of blood I had lost, there was no way that this could continue to be a viable pregnancy and he was preparing me for surgery to remove the baby. I had to deliver this news to my husband when he returned. Despite not being on a gynaecological ward, the hospital staff were great, and they gave my husband a mattress to sleep on so he could stay with me after the operation.

This time, I had complications and I needed a blood transfusion. I needed to stay in a few more nights. My husband brought my eldest daughter to see me, and we broke the news to her that I had lost another baby. Prior to discharge, I was told that there were options for what I wanted to do with my baby's remains – there would be a service, and I could attend if I wanted to. I was also given the option to write something in the book of remembrance, options I hadn't had all those years previously.

And despite some good care, as we were leaving the doctor said to me, "Well, at least we know you can get pregnant," and, "I will see you next year delivering a healthy baby." This surprised me, to say the least. I had just lost a baby, and he was treating it as if it was nothing, as if it didn't matter.

I got the same attitude at work, with comments such as, "At least it was early on, and you still have your girls," and, "Everything happens for a reason." I also realised that I hadn't started to process my first loss, all those years ago, and now here was a second one on top. This time, I sought out help, and I found a pregnancy loss support group through the Miscarriage Association, and I received counselling with a bereavement midwife through the hospital where I would have given birth, had we not lost the baby. I also contacted the charity Aching Arms, who supplied us with a teddy bear in memory of another baby – it helped to feel like I was less alone.

It took another eight months for us to decide we were ready to try again for another baby. This time I didn't even realise I was pregnant. I remember leaving my bereavement counsellor, telling her that I was going to take a pregnancy test before going to the doctors, but I believed it would be negative – only it wasn't. That was a surprise, because in the past I had always 'known' I was pregnant, but I didn't this time.

This pregnancy proceeded much like the previous one, except I had decided I didn't want any early scans. At this point, I felt that they only gave me false hope, and didn't guarantee that I would have a baby who would make it. A week or so after finding out I was pregnant, I started spotting again and having pain. I went to the doctor who said he would refer me for a scan, and, at first, I was adamant that I wasn't going – it was too hard to keep seeing a baby who wouldn't make it. He insisted I should go, though, so that we could rule out that it wasn't ectopic, so I went.

I went on my own to the scan, and this time neither a heartbeat or a foetal pole could be seen. I was taken into a side room and then left on my own for what seemed like forever, until a midwife came through to discuss the scan results. She was trying to be positive, telling me that it wasn't necessarily bad news, that I might not be as far along as I thought. It wasn't helpful. I think I snapped at her that, after five pregnancies, I knew my own body, and I knew what things should and shouldn't feel like. We scheduled in another scan for two weeks' time, but I knew in my heart of hearts that I wouldn't make that scan.

I was right. About a week or so later, on a Friday night, I started to bleed heavily, and we went to A&E again. This time, they sent me home at about 4am, but by midday on Saturday I was back. Things progressed the same way as the last pregnancy, and again I ended up in surgery, requiring a blood transfusion and, this time, IV antibiotics, too. The next time I saw my bereavement counsellor, I wasn't pregnant anymore.

I don't remember exactly when I knew that I wouldn't try again, but I do know it wasn't an easy decision, and at various points in the journey, my husband and I were on completely different pages. I think the decline in my mental health made my decision for me. The trauma of the losses led to flashbacks, panic attacks and ultimately to self-harm. It is still something I struggle with today, and at the time of writing this, I am currently on the waiting list for a hysterectomy.

I needed to write this book for two reasons: the first, to show others who have been through this journey, or are going through it, that they are not alone and that, whatever they are feeling, it is ok, no matter how dark it might seem; the second, the title of the book, to highlight that although miscarriage is so common, it shouldn't minimise the feelings that come with loss. Every person who suffers a loss is more than a statistic, and they need to be treated with care and compassion.

These poems and plays are my stories, my experiences, and I wanted to highlight that it doesn't matter when a pregnancy is lost, each loss is a loss. A woman is a mother from the day she decides to try for a baby, or when that pregnancy test turns positive. The same goes for the father. From that point, they start having hopes and dreams for their baby, and start planning their baby's future.

I wanted to show this journey, and this emotion – the rawness that can come with loss. As a result, these poems are not heavily edited. They are as I wrote them when I needed to. I don't get to edit my life to change the outcome of my pregnancies, so I didn't edit the poems.

I hope that you find comfort in these words, whatever the reason for finding my book, and I hope that if you are going through, or have gone through loss, you are not alone and you are more than a statistic.

# CHAPTER 1

## Not Just a Statistic

## More Than 1 in 4

I am not just a statistic
I am not just the one in four
Yes, I have lost my baby
But I am also something more

I may be a mother without a child
Who has no-one to whom she can turn
I was a mother to a baby
Who I couldn't carry to term

I don't have a child I can hold
But I have a loss over which I will cry
And although my baby has gone
I will never know a reason why

I am not just a statistic
I am not just the one in five
Yes, I lost my baby
And yes, I have a child who's alive

But I will still grieve my loss
For that was a loved and wanted child
They were a brother or sister
They were my baby that died

And although one child is still living
I will mourn the one who is gone
They will be forever loved
And their memory will always live on

I am not just a statistic
I am not just the one in a hundred
Yes, I have lost many babies
The reason why I have often wondered

I may have a child who is living
But I have many who have died
I never got to know any of them
There are many tears I have cried

No matter how many have come before
Each loss is a loss on its own
Each pregnancy that didn't continue
Is a baby that didn't grow

So I don't want to see the numbers
I know I have lost my child
And I have seen it in others
In their hurt they have tried to hide

So please when you see the numbers
Remember the people they represent are real
Numbers are just statistics
Not the pain that we conceal

And when you see the figures
Remember your sister, or mother, or friend
They are more than a number
And this taboo, it has to end

So please don't think just in numbers
Because nothing is ever simplistic
We are grieving families
Hidden behind the statistics

## Lost and Alone

Lost and alone,
No-one to talk to.
Lost and alone,
With no-one near.

Lost and alone,
In memories of fear.
Lost and alone,
Afraid and scared.

Lost and alone,
As no-one knows.
Lost and alone,
Is the way it stays.

## A Plea from a Bereaved Mother

Sometimes I want to talk,
to say their name
and talk about them.
Not because I want
to make you sad,
but because I need them
to be remembered and loved.

And there are times
that I will cry.
But please, don't be
afraid to talk to me
in case you upset me more,
because the worst
has already happened.

Don't avoid me in the street,
cross the road
and pretend
you can't see me,
because that hurts
more than you
can ever know.

Please remember
that I am still me.
Yes, I have changed
and will be forever.
But I'm still me,
not just the girl,
whose baby has died.

## Still a Mother

What is a mother?
She is a parent
With a child
Their source
And their origin

She gave birth
To a child
To bring up
With care
And attention

But what if…
The child died
They weren't born
Or even conceived
Is she a mother?

Yes.

She is a mother
Without a baby
To hold
To raise
And help to grow

But she loved her
She grew him

She birthed them
And then
She let them go

She didn't just miscarry
She carried a child
Who died

She may have had a stillborn
But she had a child
Who was still born

She may have made
The ultimate sacrifice
To save a child from suffering

And she may have moved
Heaven and earth
For a child who never got to be


Is she still a mother?


Yes
Always
And forever

# CHAPTER 2

## Those Six Words

## A Silent Miscarriage

As I lay down on the table, I knew what to expect.
My husband, still hopeful, reassuring but scared.
The equipment in place, switched on, all ready.
My heart is heavy, my head full of dread.
The room is silent, except in my head.
The machinery is moved, trying to find what I know.
My husband is squeezing my hand, saying all is ok,
Yet his eyes are pleading, please let it be so.
The machinery is moved, taken away.
Empty your bladder, come back.
She can't see what she needs to know.
I have confirmation, I know they have gone.
My husband, still hopeful, tells me we've done this before.
I go and I cry, knowing it is all over, and do as I am told.
I come back to a room full of silence.
Except in my head.
New machinery used, but no talking, no noise.
The room is so still, we dare not to breathe.
The longer it takes, the more I know it is true.
My husband now knowing, his eyes fill with tears.
And the silence is broken.
"I'm so sorry," she says.
She gives us a moment and leaves us alone.
We look at the screen, our baby is gone.
Where once a heartbeat visible and fast,
Now lies a stillness, a sadness so vast.
And in the room is silence, you'd hear a pin drop.
The noises in my head, gone.
True silence, at last.

## Hold On

Grasping tightly
Gripping
Holding on
Not letting go
Please
It's not
Your time
To go

But my body
Didn't get
The
Memo
As it slowly
And painfully
Expelled you
Too soon

Now gone
Lost
In a sea
Of red
Disbelieving
Unable
To just
Hold on

## I Just Had a Baby

Did I not give birth,
as my baby left
the comfort of
my womb?
That same womb
that nurtured them
and helped them grow
inside of me.

And although the
only cries to be heard
that day
were mine and mine alone,
this does not
change the fact
that they emerged,
completely separate from me.

And yet,
there is no note
of their existence,
except within my DNA,
as every pregnancy
a mother carries
leaves a trace,
a mark upon their heart.

No-one seems to realise
that I just had a baby,
as there is nothing
here to see.
Just the weighty feel
of empty arms.
And scattered all around,
the broken pieces of me.

## 'I will never forget'

Print by Emma Delgado @Idas_inkling studio

# CHAPTER 3

Just Say You're Sorry

## The Grieving Mother

Let's ignore the grieving mother
Pretend that she's not there
We don't know what to say to her
So we don't show her that we care

Let's not acknowledge her loss
What will we do if she cries?
Let's avoid her gaze
And not look her in the eyes

Let's not ask her how she is
In fact, let's not say a word
If we don't give her a voice
Then she cannot be heard

We do this because we are scared
We don't know what to say
We don't want to hurt her
We don't want to spoil her day

Yet we don't know she feels invisible
Our ignorance causes her pain
As she feels like she is an outcast
Again and again and again

We wish we could explain
Let her know she is not alone
But it is not easy
It's something that's unknown

So we both sit and suffer in silence
With her hurting more than us
Until the taboo is broken
And it is something we can discuss

## 'The Climb'

Illustration by Stacey Williamson-Michie @awesomemamaillustration

## Simply Say

I don't need to hear your stories
Of how friends did this or that
I don't need to hear it will be ok
And for you to give my arm a pat

I don't need to be told not to worry
And that will make things worse
Because I don't want to snap at you
And become sarcastic and terse

And when I tell you what's happened
And you don't know what to say
Don't tell me that I can try again
As there's always another day

And if I have children already
Please don't remind me of this
Because you're effectively saying
My lost baby, I shouldn't miss

Don't tell me it happened for a reason
Or at least it was early on
Because it doesn't change the fact
That my baby, they have gone

And don't tell me that I'll be over it
Because I will never forget
And I will always be sorry
That I'll have children I've never met

So if you're looking for something to say
Words to show you care
Then please just say you're sorry
And that you will be there

Maybe an ear to listen
Or a shoulder on which I can cry
But please don't utter platitudes
Or try to explain to me why

I'm sorry is all it takes
There doesn't need to be anything more
I'm sorry is all I need
It's all I'm asking for

**Not Invisible**

I never told you I was pregnant
That there was a baby on the way
There wasn't anything visible
Because I simply didn't say

I didn't have a baby bump
Something that you could see
I never told you of the child I carried
The mother I was about to be

And now the baby has gone
There is nothing that remains
Nothing to say that they were here
Just the lingering pain

But if you were to look closely
And find what I try to hide
You will see they did exist
They were real and then they died

I don't have any photographs
Nor any clothes or shoes
But I do have my memories
And those I cannot lose

And of course there are the dreams
And names for a girl or boy
Maybe there's that book I bought
Or the perfect little toy

And if I were to show to you
The box that is under my bed
You'll see the vest I thought they'd wear
And all the books I'd read

So I can see it clearly
The hole where they should have been
And all these things I've listed
Are ways in which they were seen

Miscarriage is not invisible
It is very much real
Something we should talk about
And something we all can feel

So please don't shy from my loss
Or pretend it didn't exist
Because they will always be my baby
And they will always be missed

Illustration by Shivani Vij @vesture_voyage

## Dads Lose Babies Too

It's not just a mother's loss
The day a baby dies
It's not just the mother's ears
That will never hear their baby's cries

It's not one heart that breaks in two
And whose eyes shed many tears
It's not one set of hopes and dreams
That have been replaced with fears

A father's heart is broken too
But he will keep this hidden
As for him to show his pain
Is something that feels forbidden

He might not break down and cry
He might be holding it together
But he too has lost a child
And that will stay with him forever

And maybe he feels torn
And doesn't quite know what to do
No doubt those who ask him how he is
Are far between and few

There may be guilt it wasn't him
That had to bear this pain
And all he could do was sit and watch
His protection was in vain

And all this makes him lonely
And feel like there is nothing he can do
As although he didn't carry the baby
Dads lose babies too

## To My Husband

I bottled some of the silence*
That was abundant in the room
After hearing those six little words;
*I'm sorry, there's no heartbeat*

I kept that bottle, and added to it,
In the hours and days that followed
When I realised I didn't need the decaf tea,
And I placed in it, the words we couldn't speak

I took it out many more times,
As I needed to talk to grieve
And you just appeared
To get up, and move on

In frustration, more silence was added
As I shared our story with others
When you couldn't say you understood
My need, and want, so share

I still carry that bottle, that silence
But not out of hurt or regret
For as I carry your silence,
I realise, I am helping to carry your grief

* 'I bottled some of the silence' after Kavya Janani

# CHAPTER 4

## What I Wish I Could Tell You

## A Request

Sometimes I hurt
And I can't explain why
And sometimes unexpectedly
I'll just sit down and cry

There is this wave of sadness
That suddenly engulfs me
And soon bleakness and darkness
Are all that I can see

The way ahead is fuzzy
Sometimes I go back in time
I get lost amidst the emotions
And feel like I'm not mine

And as much as I try to hide it
My emotions are on show
Despite the desperate, urgent need
For people not to know

So please don't ask if I'm ok
Don't ask me how I am
I will be back to a version of me
Just as soon as I can

## 'Release –Diving into hope'

Illustration by Stacey Williamson-Michie @awesomemamaillustration

## Tears

and so the tears keep falling
waiting for the day
when all the pain has faded
and completely gone away
and when the darkness is lifted
and the light at last can be seen
will I there be there to see it
or is it just another dream?

when the masks are peeled away
and all that is left is who i am
will I be a person I can come to know
or just a re-vamped me from yesterday
waiting to crumble at the first hurdle
and fall all over again?

they tell me I am strong
getting stronger everyday
they tell me I have faced life's challenges
and I am still here to tell my tale
they tell me it will get better
that it will go away
that I won't always feel like this
and the pain will fade away

how can I be strong
when I am crumbling everyday
and little by little
pieces of me are fading
slipping into the darkness
and the fear that has taken me away

I can't see tomorrow
I can't see the light
dont tell me it is out there
dont tell me I need to fight

hug me when I need you
wipe away my tears
let me know that you are there
waiting to catch me when I fall
and when I reach out to you
take my hand and hold me
stop me from fading away

## I'm Sorry

I wish I could put into words
The way that I am feeling
And tell you of the bleakness
And the thoughts I have of leaving

Of how death calls my name
In a roll call I am missing
And how I try and turn away
And pretend that I'm not listening

And how I sit and hurt myself
And make it so I cry
So in that instant I feel something
And perhaps I won't want to die

It wouldn't be a pretty letter
There'd be no laughs or smiles
But if you knew just how I was feeling
Maybe I could look you in the eyes

And I could feel your love and warmth
Which would help soothe these fears inside
And I would have you next to me
The next time that I need to cry

But this is just too dark
It's not something of which is spoken
And so I sit here on my own
Alone and feeling broken

And if the day does come
When death calls and I am listening
I am sorry that you didn't know
I am sorry that I'm now missing

The reasons I can't tell you
Are far too many to list
But know that I'll always love you
And you will always be missed

## I'm Tired

I'm tired of being the weak one
The one that will always cry
I'm tired of feeling I'll never be happy
No matter how hard I try

I'm sick of feeling needy
Of always feeling sad
These thoughts inside my head
That are slowly driving me mad

I can't cope with the endless questions
The what ifs and what might have been
I hate that my grief is invisible
And sometimes I just want to be seen

I'm scared that those around me
Will see me for less than I am
And will focus on what I can't do
Rather than on what I can

I feel like I have been lost
A piece discarded each time
And I'll never regain those pieces
Which once were mine

My heart is hurting and heavy
And there's an empty hole inside
I've gone deep inside myself
As it's somewhere safe to hide

And although I know I can cry
And I don't have to try so hard
I'm tired of pretending
I'm tired of being on guard

But I'm sorry I feel guilty
For taking up all of your time
I am sorry I am spreading my sadness
Instead of keeping what is mine

Believe me I want to be normal
Whatever that may be
But just stay with me a little longer
Until what that is, I can finally see

## My Apologies

I'm sorry I am going to have to lie to you
I will tell you I'm ok
That things have improved
And that the darkness is getting lighter
With each passing day

And I'll practise my smile
So it looks real and true
But even as I do it
I'll know no matter what
It won't quite reach my eyes

I won't tell you that I cried
And that my heart is broken in two
I can't tell you of my pain
Of how it's just too hard
To get up and keep on going

I won't let you see that I'm broken
As it's too much for you to take
And I won't tell you of my fears
Or show you my scars
Because I want to save you

Save you from my pain and hurt
And from the belief you need to help me
Shelter you from my world
Protect you so you don't walk away
When I'm too much to bear

It's because I love you
I care for and value you
That when you ask me how I am
The only answer I can give you
Is honestly, I'm doing ok

Illustration by Sophie Cook @doodley.bobz

## I Don't Want to Lie

I covered up my scars today
I deliberately hid them away
I couldn't look at the multiple scars
And I didn't want to lie
Or be asked about what they were
And how they came to be there

So instead I lied to myself
By covering them up
With bandages meant for my eczema
I wear these all the time
No questions to be asked
Instead, just a visible lie

And I will lie if I am asked
If my skin is bad or has flared again
And I will lie if I am asked
If I am ok today
I will lie again and again
Because I cannot tell the truth

## Not Strong

They say I am strong
I am not
I feel myself crumbling
Falling
And slowly slipping away

Not strong
But weak
Falling at each hurdle
Waiting
For it to be over
For it to stop
For it to end

Not strong
Just tired
Tired of playing
This game of life
Of wanting
And waiting
For the music to stop

Not strong
Just empty
Nothing left inside
A hollow shell
Battered and broken
Shadowy remains
Of the person I used to be

Not strong
Just me
Doing what needs to be done
Surviving
Yet at the same time
Slowly dying

**Broken**

I'm broken
Trying to pick up
The pieces on the floor
And I'm hurting
Some more

The pain doesn't leave me
Just lessens in time
I want to be the person
I was before

Not tired of fighting
And crying and breaking
But whole and complete
With a little new person to meet

I need something to hold on to
Not something to pick me up
From this place on the floor
And a light shining somewhere
To brighten the bleakness
That constantly knocks at my door

I don't like this strength
That keeps pulling me through
And how I wish
I never needed to know
That I could be broken

Again and again
But still find the strength
To find my way through

And when all the pieces
Are picked up and rebuilt
There'll always be
A missing piece
That will forever be
In the shape of you

And I'll still be fragile
And glued together
Just waiting to break
With each little shake
That knocks me again
To the floor


Waiting to be picked up
And mended and glued
And knowing that
Despite being broken
I will make it through
Time and time again

# CHAPTER 5

## Time

## My Time

They say in time it will get better
In time things will change
In time it will be different
In time the pain you feel is less
In time

But what time?
Whose time?
And when?

The seconds of time
That pass by in the instant, so slowly
That you reach out to stop them
And in that same instant it is done
Gone
Lost
In time

Or the time that is a minute
A lifetime so it seems
But really all that time has gone
Lost in the blink of an eye
In time
Gone

Or is that time an hour?
So much you have aged
So much you have learned
So much that has gone
In time everlasting
Ever fading
Ever fleeting
Forever gone
Lost
In time

Is time counted in the days?
The weeks
The months that follow on
Knowing, counting, yet disbelieving

All that time has gone
Knowing how much has changed
And yet how much more has stayed the same?
How much has passed?
How much has gone?
In time

And yet the years go by
Memories fade
New ones grow
And you realise things got better
Things changed slowly
In time

Maybe in an instant
That was a second long ago
Maybe in a lifetime lived in only a day
And maybe it was the eternity of time
Passed by from now and the moment of yesterday

So much lost
So much gained
So much changed
Yet so much stayed the same
In time

Whose time?
What time?
And when?

In my time

The time that I am ready
Ready to say goodbye
Ready to live again
Ready to let go of the pain

So tell them it takes my time
However long that takes

## I'll Never Be Over You

I shouldn't be broken
I shouldn't need fixed
Time should have cured me of this

I shouldn't keep crying
And hurting and sighing
I should be over this

And it's not like I knew you
Or held you
Or saw you

You were a dream
My imagination
Not something tangible or real

And yet my love for you
And this space where you were
Is still here

I shouldn't be broken
I shouldn't need fixed
Time should have cured me of this

I shouldn't keep crying
Or hurting or sighing
I should be over this

There shouldn't be reminders
Of what could have been
Life is just what it is

And I have the others
The ones who are here
I shouldn't miss you the way that I do

And I shouldn't be broken
And I shouldn't need fixed
Time should have cured me of this

They say I shouldn't keep crying
Or hurting or sighing
They say I should be over this

But you were my baby
My son or my daughter
The child I will always miss

And I love you and need you
I miss you and want you
But you will always be gone

So maybe I am broken
And maybe I need to be fixed
And time will cure me of this

And I will keep crying
And hurting and sighing
But I'll never be over this

For this is my child
My son or my daughter
This was a child of mine

And this needs to be grieved for
And remembered and loved
And not just something dismissed

This isn't something
That can be forgotten
And time can't wash it away

And I might still cry
And I will still hurt and maybe I'll sigh
But I won't ever forget
No, I won't ever forget

## Paused

I never realised how much
My life had been put on hold
Or just when I clicked pause
And time just seem to slow

We've seen summers and winters
And autumns and springs
And yet I've got nothing new
Nor nothing different to show

I'm at the proverbial crossroads
Only there's no map to show me the way
It's a decision that is mine to make
Mine, and mine alone

I hate the choice that I've been given
As no answer is right or wrong
And even if we try again
I could still be left here, stuck in time

And although life seems to have stopped
The hands of time go round
I age and get older and older
While the dream remains the same

And how do I un-pause life
And make it go round again?
Do I give up the dream and the hope
And say we'll never try again?

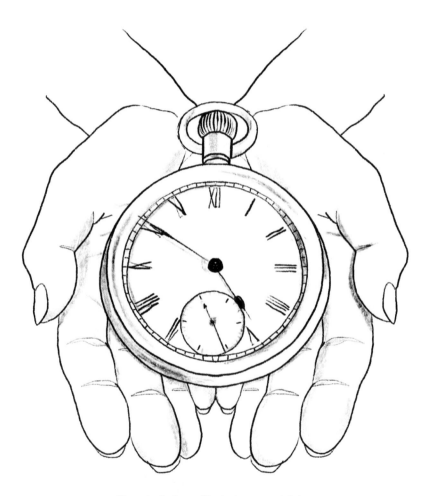

Illustration by Joanne Chard @joanneamandadesigns

## Time to Sing a Different Song

Time still works its magic
As days turn into nights
And summer sun makes way
For rainy autumn days

And the calendar page still turns
To mark a brand-new day
As the birdsong softly changes
Until the song just floats away

The music will keep playing
Although it plays a different song
And the story is still written
It just tells a different tale

And the world, it just forgets
As a mark was never made
A footprint never created
So it couldn't be washed away

And the memory never changes
Never grows and never turns old
In a world that is still turning
It constantly remains the same

And somewhere in the middle
There is one who can't move on
Stuck between the hands of time
Trapped, as time goes on

And time doesn't work its magic
They're far beyond time's reach
Frozen in a time and place
That never knew their worth

So should the page turn over?
Should they sing a different song?
Or should time just ignore them?
And should time just move on?

## A Different Tomorrow

tears are forever falling
to hide this pain I feel
if somehow I don't say it
then maybe it's not real

if I could only hide away
somewhere far and wide
where no one would ever find me
then I'd argue that I'd tried

I'd say I tried to ask for help
but the words they wouldn't come
I'd say I tried to face it all
but it will never be over and done

I'd ask them what the point was
of turning it over and over again
reliving the memories of yesterday
and reliving all the pain

and then they'd see I am sure
I am doing what is best
at last I'm putting me first
instead of all the rest

and right now all I want
is to go and hide again
somewhere in the distance
where I will feel no pain

I don't want to live with tears
I don't want to feel this sorrow
so if I go and hide away
maybe I'll have a different tomorrow

# CHAPTER 6

Pregnancy After Loss

## Wiping

Each and every
Time I wipe
I check the
Toilet paper
Searching
For those early
Tell-tale signs
And I breathe
A somewhat
Temporary
Sigh of relief
As I realise
That for now
Everything may
Just be ok

## A Moment in Time

Just a picture
A snapshot in time
Not a certainty
Of a different outcome

A snapshot in time
A pause, a moment, a hope
Of a different outcome
But not a guarantee

A pause, a moment, a hope
A glimmer of what could be
But not a guarantee
Only just, a maybe

A glimmer of what could be
Just a picture
Only just, a maybe
Not a certainty

**Trying Again**

There are times and seasons
When I feel your loss more than others
When I wonder whether you were
A sister or a brother

And instead of a child to hold
I watch a candle and its flame
Flickering in the darkness
Marking a baby without a name

And then I sit and wonder
What if we tried again?
How much love we still have to give?
And how much we have to gain?

But I know I'm not guaranteed
To bring a baby home
And I'm not sure I've got the strength
To leave hospital alone … again

I've already got three candles
Which are three too many to light
And I'm not sure I can face a fourth
I'm not sure I can fight the fight

I can dream of what might be
But my hope, I fear it has gone
So I must face the fact
That my future children may be none

I'm not sure I've got the answer
Or if I ever will truly know
Just please don't ask me the question
*Will you ever have any more?*

It's far too loaded a question
With an answer I don't have to give
Because I've got no guarantee
That I'll have a baby who'll live

## Pregnancy After Loss

Most mothers plan
To bring their babies home
To hold them in their arms
To look them in their eyes
And to love them
They don't plan for them to die

Their pregnancy is full of hope
And dreams of what will be
And although there is uncertainty
And will it be a girl or boy
It's not fear and darkness at their door
But light and lots of joy

I wish I had that hope
And how I dream it hadn't gone
That each pregnancy was a baby
Which would grow and I'd bring home
But loss has taken that away from me
Where once was hope, there's none

Replaced by fear and panic
No dreams of what will be
But nightmares of the ending
Of how and when and where
And of the empty arms I'll have
And no baby for which to care

So, although I'd rather my baby live
I know there's no guarantee
Pregnancy doesn't always mean a baby
Will be coming home with me
Sometimes I have to say goodbye
And let my child fly free

So, although I don't want to plan for it
It's always in my thoughts
And I'm scared to dream of a baby
Of one which I will hold
Because empty arms are heavy
And empty arms grow cold

So don't think of me as morbid
For thinking my baby will die
This is my truth, my reality
The only thing that I know
And as much as I want my baby to stay
I must also prepare for them to go

**Fear**

A burning deep inside,
Frantic, frequent, frightening,
Quick, quiet breathing.

A glint in the eye,
Showing the darks and depths
Of the heart.

The voices in the head,
Conflicting and confronting,
Mainly confusing.

Hidden away, slouched,
No confidence,
Overpowering feelings.

Fear,
Powerful, possessive, persistent.

It hurts.

Angela Marshall

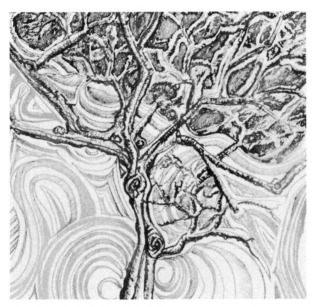

Illustration by Lottie Bolster @lottie_bolster

# CHAPTER 7

When the Trying Stops

## When the Trying Stops

I didn't expect to come so far then stop
For things to end this way
I guess I had just always hoped
That there'd be another baby some day

But it doesn't feel like giving up
Nor do I think I've failed
And just to add a platitude
It's not that the ship has sailed

It's just this journey has not been easy
And it really has taken its toll
My body has taken a battering,
Alongside my mind, my heart and soul

I've opened and closed this door
So many times before
But it needs to stay shut now
As I can't do this anymore

By keeping it ajar
I was keeping the hope alive
But there was also a bleakness
In knowing a baby might die

It's not been an easy decision
One I wish I hadn't had to make
My heart is still hurting and aching
But my mind knows what it can take

And I must accept my story
Has an ending I didn't intend
But perhaps now I can start to heal
And my heart, it can start to mend

But it doesn't mean forgetting
And it never ever will
It just means learning to live with loss
And the gap that I'll never fill

## After a Storm

There isn't always a calmness
In the time that follows a storm
The skies don't suddenly clear
And a rainbow isn't formed

Sometimes, there is only hope
That a calmness can be found
To come to terms with learning
To live with what we have

We may have empty arms
A child we never held
Not knowing the bittersweet sadness
Of a nurturing a baby after loss

Or maybe we held our baby's hand
And wept our final goodbyes
As they were taken from us
And we were forced to walked a different path

And for those of us with children
It doesn't change the feelings
Of the storm we carry within
Or the search for the rainbow in the sky

As those rainbows are beacons of hope
A sign of what could be
A wish we carry deep inside
But sadly, there is no guarantee

So don't tell me that there's a rainbow
Because sometimes, there's just not
And to tell us that there is
Just fills us with false hope

There isn't always a rainbow
That follows every storm
Sometimes there's just a stillness
And perhaps a wish upon a star

Illustration by Bethany Field @bethany_field_art

## The Last Time

If I'd have known it was the last time
That I'd carry a baby to term
Would I have done things differently?
Perhaps made many more memories?
Would I have taken more pictures
With bump, my husband and daughter?

If I'd have known that last breastfeed
Would be the last one ever,
Maybe I'd have taken time to enjoy it
Or perhaps have fed for longer?
Instead of thinking there'd be a time
When I'd have another

And for the first few years
Before I knew she was my last
I wonder if it would have changed things
What I did and how I felt
If I would have cherished it more
And not how I'd do things differently

Now those lasts are painful
As I'm acutely aware
That there'll not be another first
Everything is my last
From that first word and step
To the first lost tooth and day of school

As I know there are no more
I think about things differently
And I wish I would have known
As that last pregnancy
Was the start of many lasts
That didn't end with a last baby

## Saying Goodbye

I've said goodbye to you
In far too many ways
When the words 'I'm Sorry'
Were first spoken
And we left hospital in a daze

And then again in theatre
With tears falling from my eyes
And again in the pain and hurt
That can only be known
When a baby dies

I said goodbye to you on the pier
As I imagined you float away
And I've said it again and again
As I've imagined you growing
Day after day after day

I said it when I said I'd stop counting
And marking how old you'd be
It didn't mean I was forgetting
It didn't mean I was moving on
As you will always be remembered by me

And I said it when I said I'd stop trying
I've said it for the baby that never was
I said it to the dreams, the ifs
And to the what might have beens
And I've simply said it just because

And I say it now when I tidy
And rehome what should have been yours
From the clothing I desperately hung on to
To the highchair that called to be used
Otherwise they'd be dust catchers forever more

And this goodbye it seems final
As I am saying you will never be here
Even though you clearly are
But I don't think it will be last one
No matter how final it seems

# CHAPTER 8

## Life After Loss

## Due Date

Today would have been the day
I held you in my arms
Looked into your eyes
And heard your sweet cries

I would know your name
And who you are
Count your fingers and toes
See your soft squishy nose

And although I'd be tired
And probably in pain
It would be worth it
Things would be perfect

Just to have you here
Close to me
But life had other plans
It was not meant to be

So today I hold you
In my heart
I still carry you with me
We're never apart

Angela Marshall

I'll never know why
You were taken too soon
Why you didn't grow
Why you couldn't bloom

You'll be my butterfly
Who far too early
Spread your wings
And learnt to fly

But you'll always be mine
You'll never be gone
Never left far behind
Never far from my mind

Illustration by Rachel Dickens @lollysnow

## Counting

I promised I'd stop counting
As I can't do it anymore
Marking dates and milestones
If only you'd continued to grow

It doesn't mean I'm forgetting
Or pretending you weren't here
As I carry your memory with me
And I know you are always near

It's just it gets too painful thinking
Of the ifs and what could have been
And imagining what life would be like
If you were here and you were seen

Instead you're something missing
A gap where a child should be
The empty space in the photograph
Who should be sitting next to me

But I find that as time moves on
And the days and months go by
I know the age you would have been
If you hadn't learnt to fly

So although I don't keep counting
I know that somehow I always will
Because you will always be missing
A gap that I can never fill

And no matter how many years pass
I will always know your age
As you are part of my book of life
And you deserve your page

Illustration by Rachel Dickens @lollysnow

## Snow

Snow fell today
I wish I could see your reaction
Would you have loved it
Like your middle sister?
Or been scared and unsure
Just as your big sister was?

Would you have put your hand out
To try and catch each flake
As It fell?
Would you have snuggled your head
Into my chest to hide
From this strange thing in the air?

I'm sure your sisters
Would have taken your hands
And walked with you
Your feet
Making tiny footprints
As you took your baby steps

And they'd have help you
Build the best snowman
That we'd ever seen
But I am sure there would be
Tears and tantrums
As he slowly melted

Angela Marshall

But instead all I have
Are dreams and what ifs
A lot of what could have beens
Which flutter away and melt
As each and every snowflake
Slowly disappears

Until the ground is clear again
With no sign of the snow
Which fell
And came and touched my heart
However brief that was
And went away again

Illustration by Rachel Dickens @lollysnow

## Missing

I see you today
In the spaces
Where you
Should have been

In the missing
First photograph
And the birthday cards
That never got to be sent

There's no celebration today
No party, no cake
No recognition
That you ever were

But you were, and you are
As I carry you in my heart
And you are my little butterfly
Another one, who flew away

# To My Missing Babies

## Due: 16th July 2008

Joined together, connected
United, hearts beating as one
Lasting for a time, cut short
Yearning to hold you, my child

## Due: 29th May 2017

Month you should be due
Alive, not just a memory
Years just passing by

## Due: 1st February 2018

Frozen in time
Ever the same
Briefly here, then gone
Released, with wings to fly
Unrelenting questions
Asking, simply, why?
Remembered. Loved.
Yet lost.

# CHAPTER 9

## The Immense Grief of Loss

## The Waves of Grief

It comes to me in waves
Some stronger than before
And threatens to engulf me
Or knock me to the floor

There are those days
When it surprises me
Turns me blind
And it's all that I can see

And the days I see it coming
When I try to face it eye to eye
But it doesn't change the outcome
I still breakdown and cry

And most days I feel empty
There's a hole inside my heart
There's a piece that's missing
And you're that missing part

You were never lost
Although I know you can't be found
I feel that you are with me
That you will always be around

And when that wave comes
As it inevitably will
I'll not try to run and hide from it
I shall try to stand tall and still

I'll let the wave embrace me
And perhaps sweep me off my feet
Until the day that they don't hurt
The day that again we meet

Illustration by Amanda Clarke @amandaclarke_illustration

## My Children

I've lost who I am
As I sit here and cry
And weep for the child
That'll I never know
The hand never held
The one who didn't grow

I'm still a mother
I've children to hold
Yet my heart still aches
For the one who had to go
To a place I can't see
And who I can never know

And platitudes come
They're somewhere safe
Too good for this earth
Safely away from harm
Yet where could be better
Than in their mother's arm?

She was here for a moment
He was gone in a second
Yet they lived
And they breathed
Within our hearts
And in our dreams

And though the world moves on
And everyone has forgotten
No matter the distance
No matter how far
I'm a mother to five children;
Two living, three stars

## My Idea of You

I'll never see your little face
Nor know your tiny hands
I'll never count ten tiny toes
Or see your squishy nose

I'll have to imagine your smile
The twinkle in your eyes
I'll only know you sleeping
I'll never hear your cries

I'll dream of your newness
Your new-born baby smell
The colour that your hair would be
And whether you'd resemble me

I'll see you in our family photos
In the one who isn't there
And I will always love you
Though your loss will never seem fair

I'll never know who you would be
The person you'd grow into
But I'll see you in my dreams
In my idea of you

## New Shoes

I picked up an old pair of shoes today.
They used to be comfortable shoes
That took me on a journey
Without taking a detour.
But those shoes,
They don't fit anymore.

Today I walk a different path
And I wear some other shoes.
I never wanted these ones.
I didn't pick these out at all.
But now that I've worn them once
I know I'll wear them forever more.

These shoes are cold, ugly and heavy
But I know that I won't take them off.
And as much as I liked my old shoes,
I couldn't go back to them now.
I'll forever walk in my new shoes.
I'll walk on this path of loss.

## Some Days

There are days when the pain is too heavy
And your memory too hard to hold
When everything is a reminder
And the tears just start to fall

But I can't just put you down
And forget you for a while
As the pain lies in my heart
Behind my eyes and in my smile

And each footstep feels like a marathon
A journey too hard to walk
And life feels like a burden
A subject of which we don't talk

And although I carry this on my own
As there is no one to shoulder this load
I don't think I would change it
No matter how much I want to fold

So I continue to carry you with me
And some days are lighter than others
But know I will never forget you
No matter how much the darkness smothers

And when the dark days come
I will look for you in the sun's rays
Riding on the breeze of the wind
And I'll carry you all of my days

## Grief

Calm and serene, as the waves lap the shore
A gentleness, which maybe wasn't there before
But then something changes, something unseen
And the waves have a new quality, vicious and mean

And higher and stronger, they grow and they grow
Gathering strength, speed, height and more
Not knowing, nor caring, what it leaves in its wake
As it crashes back down, in its final break

There's a beauty and a peace to hearing the noise
A majestic quality, its own distinctive poise
But there's also destruction and pain left behind
As structures crumble, become less defined

And they engulf and suffocate those trapped inside
A weight hard to manage, a cry never cried
And the power of the waves, it's hard to ignore
Because once it has gone, it will come once more

You may look out to sea and see not the waves
Nor the destruction left in its watery graves
Yet the memory of the pain, although it has faded
Leaves the love of the sea and its joy slightly jaded

As no sooner do you turn and start to walk away
Does it catch you unguarded, and knock you astray
And the tears that you cried and thought that were gone
Come back with the sadness that makes it hard to move on

And as you wade through the waves, the grief and the tears
The darkness around you, playing on your fears
The wave starts to break, its power is broken
And the battle between you are words left unspoken

Because you are not naïve, you know it will return
And when it does, you will feel it hurt and it burn
But then it will pass and eventually you two will part
Until all that remains, is the memory in your heart

# CHAPTER 10

## The Plays

# Simply Say – The Play

### Scene One

*Radio recording:*

And our last message of the night comes from Sarah, who has an important message to share about a particular type of grief. I'll read it out now for you:

"I have heard that grief is grief. It doesn't matter who it was and how you knew them. It's ok to hurt and it's ok to cry. People are understanding, and they ask how you are, how you feel, what they can do to help. Until, of course, grief isn't grief anymore.

"I have learnt that miscarriage grief is a different kind of grief, especially if it was an early loss. Then grief isn't grief. It doesn't matter what the doctors say, or the nurses, the counsellors or the websites – that each person is individual and it is ok to grieve for as long as it takes – not when you live in reality.

"Everyone expects you to be upset at first, but when that grief lasts months, it's suddenly not ok. When you are caught breaking down over a colleague's new baby four months after your loss, you feel as if you should be over it. And when your due date comes around and you still aren't pregnant again and your arms feel empty and heavy, society says that we should be ok with it.

I have come to realise that people think it is ok to ask if it still upsets you, or are you not over it yet? And if you have living children, at least you still have children to love.

"Yet miscarriage grief is different, apparently. It's like it's not real grief. And the guilt and shame we feel when we get upset, grieve our loss, is indescribable. It is like the world expects us to move on and forget. Our grief isn't real.

"Only it was. It is. Grief is grief and it matters.

"Miscarriage matters.

"Our babies mattered."

Well, that certainly leaves us with a lot to think about. Good evening, and thanks for listening.

*Radio crackle.*

### Scene Two

*Lucy enters. She is talking on her mobile phone.*

Lucy:     Yes, yes, I will call you if I need you. I am sure it will be fine. It's just going to be hard, that's all. Mmm. I know it's only been three weeks but I need to get back to into a routine. I'll be fine. I'll call you later. Love you, too. Bye.

*Curtains open to reveal an office type situation, with office clock shown, with two desks set on either side. Lucy enters her office*

*Lucy looks at her phone, delaying going into work. As she does this, Evelyn enters from stage left. She is also talking on her mobile phone.*

**Evelyn:**          **I wish you could have driven me to work.**
**Yes, I know it's been three weeks. Ok, ok. Well please just tell me I can ring you if I need you? I'm not asking you to drop everything, I just need to know that you're there. Ok, ok. Fine. I'll be fine. I'll call you later. Bye.**

*Evelyn shoves her phone straight into her bag, looking visibly distressed after her phone call, and tries to compose herself.*

*None scripted interaction between Lucy and Evelyn as first time they have seen each other since their losses.*

*As both get settled and sit down, their Colleague and Manager enter office.*

Colleague:     Lucy, you're back. (Gives Lucy a hug). I'm so sorry to hear about your mum. How are you doing?

Lucy:     I'm ok. It's been hard, but I think I need to get back to normal.

Manager:     Do you need to have a chat about anything or are you ready to just jump back in?

Lucy:     I'll be ok. I think I just need to jump back in and see how things go. Thanks for the call last week though, to check on me and what I needed. That was really touching.

Manager:     No problems. You know where I am if you need me.

Lucy:     Thanks.

*Lights fade down, not to complete black out but quite low, on Lucy's side of the stage to highlight Evelyn. Evelyn is struggling being back at work. She randomly checks her emails but picks up her phone, too. At one point she sits with her head in her hands.*

*Colleague walks through the office and, although Evelyn tries to get their attention, they deliberately don't look at her. Evelyn is visibly hurt by this.*

*Manager comes in and goes to Evelyn. Manager looks visibly uncomfortable, as if they don't know what to say.*

Manager:        Evelyn, lovely to see you back…
                Erm, I'll leave you to catch up on what you have missed.

*Manager walks away as Evelyn goes to say something. Evelyn visibly shrinks back into her chair.*

*Music to indicate passing of time, both Evelyn and Lucy act out answering the phone or typing emails*

### Scene Three
*Music fades and we see Lucy and Colleague at Lucy's desk*

Colleague:      Well, I think it's time for a cuppa, don't you?

Lucy:           Yeah, I suppose so.

*Move to back of stage, centre, where there is a kettle, cups, tea bags etc.*

Colleague:      So, how has your first day back been so far?

Lucy:           It's been good. People haven't been afraid to talk to me about
                Mum, and I am pleased. It's not like I want to talk about her all
                the time, but it's nice that people have asked me how I am.
                I've appreciated it.

Colleague:      That's good. It's hard to know the right thing to say, isn't it?
                When someone has a bereavement.

Lucy:           You'd be surprised – sometimes, just saying 'I'm sorry' is enough.
                *(Pause for thought.)* I think I'll take this back to my desk.

| | |
|---|---|
| Colleague: | See you later for lunch? |
| Lucy: | Yeah, no problem. |

*As Lucy sits back down, Manager comes to talk to her and Evelyn goes over to make a cup of tea. She bumps into Colleague.*

**Evelyn:** **Sorry, I didn't see you there.**

Colleague: No problem, it's fine.

*There is an awkward silence as neither of them knows what to say.*

Colleague: So … how have you been?

**Evelyn:** **You know, up and down. It's still hard to process.**

Colleague: I can't even imagine what you are going through.
I didn't even know you were pregnant.

**Evelyn:** **No, well, not many people did. It was quite early on, really.**

Colleague: Oh well, that's a blessing in disguise, isn't it? I mean, it's not really a baby in the early stages. (She realises what she is saying and tries to make it better.) I mean, if you'd lost it later, that would be harder. A friend's sister lost her baby at 34 weeks. T
hat was terrible. It was her first baby, as well.

**Evelyn:** **Yeah, I guess…**

Colleague: At least you've still got your two girls at home – just remember that. *(Pause as Evelyn looks like she's going to cry.)*
Anyway, I'd best take this back to my desk…

*Colleague hurries off stage. Evelyn is visibly distressed, almost (if not) in tears.*

**Evelyn:** *(almost a whisper to Colleague, who has already gone)*
**But they were a baby. They were my baby, and they've gone, and I miss them…**

*Evelyn visibly breaks down in tears. As she goes back to her desk, Manager looks over at her but then goes back to talking to Lucy. Evelyn opens up her blog on her computer, we see the words appear, and a voiceover says the words as they are typed.*

VOICEOVER: I went back to work today. It's been hard. I know people don't know what to say, but I feel like I have been ignored. I've seen people deliberately walk the other way and not talk to me. I get that they don't know what to say, I really do, but not saying anything is like another stab through my heart.

Someone told me today that I should be grateful it wasn't a baby yet. Of course it was a baby. It was a baby from the moment I found out I was pregnant, and now it's gone. I haven't just lost my baby, I've lost my hopes and my dreams for that baby. My children have lost a brother or a sister.

They actually told me to be grateful that I still had children at home – as if that makes everything better. Oh, don't worry that you lost a baby, you have two at home, so it doesn't matter. I bet no one says that to someone who has lost a sibling. Well, you still have two brothers, so be grateful.

Maybe I came back too soon. I don't know. It's been three weeks. I should be feeling better, but I'm not. It never gets easier. No matter how many losses, it never gets easier.

*Evelyn goes back to work. As she does, the telephone on Lucy's desk rings.*

Lucy: *(answering phone)* Hello, Lucy speaking, how can I help? Oh Jane, hi. Yes, it has been a while since we have spoken. I had to take some time off. No, not a holiday, bereavement leave. My mum. Thank you, but that's ok, you didn't know. No, no, I am fully up to speed. Yeah, I know what's been happening in my absence. Yeah, I've been fully caught up. No problem. I'll look at getting that over to you later today. Honestly, it's ok. Speak to you soon. Bye.

*The phone on Evelyn's desk rings. She looks at it like it will bite her and can't answer it. After a momentor two, Colleague comes through with a bit of paper and gives it to Evelyn. She walks away without saying a word.*

**Evelyn:** *(with a heavy sigh)* **Great. Just what I need.** *(She picks up the phone and dials.)* **Hi Barbara, it's Evelyn. I'm just returning your call. Well, no, I am not sure what's been happening over the past few weeks. No, I haven't been in the office. No, I've been off sick. No, erm, I ... I ... It's complicated. No, no, I'm fine honestly. Yeah, I can calculate her maternity. Just send me over the MATb1. Yeah. And I'll get caught up on the other stuff, too. No problem. I'll email it all over later. Thanks. Bye.** *(She puts the phone down.)* **Stupid bloody maternity pay!** *(She sits with her head in her hands.)*

*Music to indicate passing of time, both Evelyn and Lucy act out answering the phone or typing emails, etc.*

## Scene Four

| | |
|---|---|
| Colleague: | It's time for lunch. Are you coming out, Lucy? |
| Lucy: | Yeah, why not. It'll be nice to get out of the office for a while. |
| Manager: | Shall we just go and sit out the front rather than be cooped up inside? It's a lovely day. Would be a shame to miss what little good weather we have. |
| Lucy: | Good idea. Evelyn, are you coming? |
| **Evelyn:** | **Oh, I don't know. I was just going to stay here and catch up on some emails.** |
| Lucy: | Come on, it will do you the world of good to get out of the office. |
| **Evelyn:** | *(hesitant)* **I'm really not sure** |
| Lucy: | *(goes over to Evelyn)* Come on, some fresh air will do you good. |

*All sit in front of the 'office'. Evelyn sits off to one side, so you're not sure if she's sitting with the other three or not.*

| | |
|---|---|
| Manager: | So how has your first day back been, Lucy? |
| Lucy: | It's been great. Everyone has been really great. To think I was worried about coming back and what people would say. I needn't have wasted that time. |
| Colleague: | I didn't even know your mum was ill. |
| Lucy: | Neither did we. It was all really sudden. She went in for some tests as she'd been feeling tired and lost a lot of weight and they diagnosed the cancer almost immediately. There was nothing that ould be done though and she went downhill quite quickly. |

Colleague: That's terrible.

Lucy: I'm not sure which is worse. That it happened so fast and we barely had a chance to process it or if it was prolonged and she would have been in pain and waiting to die. It's hard and I get angry, wishing she was still here and we had more time together, but then I remember that others don't get the time that we had, and I should be grateful.

Manager: Oh Lucy, you shouldn't compare yourself to others. It doesn't matter how long you had your mum for, she was still your mum, and you are allowed to grieve for as long as it takes.

Lucy: Thanks. (*Pause while Lucy realised that Evelyn hasn't spoken in a while.*) Evelyn, come and sit a bit closer
(*Evelyn moves a tiny bit.*)

Lucy: So how has your first day back been?

**Evelyn:** **Oh, you know. Similar to yours.**

Lucy: Really?

**Evelyn:** **Yeah, everyone is trying to say the right things.**

Colleague: I hadn't realised how common miscarriage was.
They say that one in four pregnancies in a miscarriage.
I didn't realise that.

**Evelyn:** **Yeah, most people don't. And of those, another 20% will have another one.**

Colleague: Really? I don't know if I could face another pregnancy after a miscarriage. You're not going to try again, are you, Evelyn?

**Evelyn:** **Erm, well it's still early days and we haven't made any decisions yet.**

Colleague: I wouldn't if I was you. I mean you were hospitalised again this time, weren't you? It can't be good for the kids seeing you go through this each time.

| Lucy: | I think we should change the subject. What's everyone's plans for the weekend? I know it's only Monday, but we need something to look forward to, eh? Olivia? |

Lucy: I think we should change the subject. What's everyone's plans for the weekend? I know it's only Monday, but we need something to look forward to, eh? Olivia?

Manager: I'm off on a spa day with the girls.

Lucy: Sounds lovely. I don't think I've ever been on a spa day.

Manager: Y ou really should. They are really relaxing, and, well – you only live once. *(Phone rings.)* Oh sorry, I should take this…

Colleague: I'm off to my niece's fourth birthday party. She keeps asking when me and James are getting married. I'm sure he thinks I'm putting it up to her.

**Evelyn:** **That's kids for you. My four-year-old is getting married to her best friend at school and they are getting a cat. She has it all planned out.**

Colleague: So, what about you? What are you up to?

**Evelyn:** **We're off to the pizza and prosecco festival. I haven't been out for a drink since…**

*(Manager walks back over and re-joins the conversation.)*

Manager: Oh, that sounds nice. And it'll be good that you can have a drink again. I can't imagine anything worse than being sober and surrounded by drunk people.

**Evelyn:** **I think I'm gonna head back inside… thanks for inviting me out to lunch.**

*Evelyn rushes out, visibly upset.*

Lucy: Oh god girls! You might as well have told her that her grief didn't matter.

Manager: Excuse me?

Colleague: What? Did we say something insensitive?

Lucy: Never mind, I'm going to check that she's ok. I'll see you back inside.

*Lucy packs up her things and follows Evelyn. Manager and Colleague follow after.*

### Scene Five
*Spotlight centre stage for a moment of reflection*

*Evelyn comes and stands in the spotlight.*

**Evelyn:**    *(mimicking)* **'Oh at least it was early on'; 'At least you've still got your kids'; 'One in bloody four'.**

I am not only a statistic
I am not just the one in four
Yes, I have lost my baby
But I am also something more

I may be a mother without a child
Who has no one to which she can turn
I was a mother to a baby
Who I couldn't carry to term

I don't have a child I can hold
But I have a loss over which I will cry
And although my baby has gone
I will never know a reason why

I am not only a statistic
I am not just the one in five
Yes, I lost my baby
And yes, I have a child who's alive

But I will still grieve my loss
For that was a loved and wanted child
They were a brother or sister
They were my baby that died

And although one child is still living
I will mourn the one who is gone
They will be forever loved
And their memory will always live on

I am not only a statistic

I am not just the one in a hundred
Yes, I have lost many babies
The reason why I have often wondered

I may have a child who is living
But I have many who have died
I never got to know any of them
There are many tears I have cried

No matter how many have come before
Each loss is a loss on its own
Each pregnancy that didn't continue
Is a baby that didn't grow

So I don't want to see the numbers
I know I have lost my child
And I have seen it in others
In their hurt they have tried to hide

So please when you see the numbers
Remember the people they represent are real
Numbers are only statistics
Not the pain that we conceal

*Evelyn breaks down in tears and sobs on the floor. Lucy enters and goes to Evelyn.*

Lucy:          Oh Evelyn, come here. *(Hugs her.)*
               Why didn't you say things were so bad?

**Evelyn:       I couldn't. My loss feels like it's not as important as yours. It
seems silly – I didn't even get to know my baby – I was just 7 weeks along… It felt
               like too much to put on you.**

Lucy:          Don't be daft. I'm here for you anytime,
               and besides, you've had a loss, too.

**Evelyn:       Thanks.**

Lucy:          You shouldn't need to be worried about your entitlement to grieve.
               You haven't just lost anything. A loss is a loss, and there is no 'just'
               about it. Anyway, you knew what you were getting when you got
               pregnant – having the two girls at home. You would probably
               have had a baby that was the double of the two you already have

and I bet you had them slotted into holidays and photos and weddings and everything.

**Evelyn:** **I hadn't thought about it like that.**

Lucy: We lost a baby last year, too. I was about 12 weeks pregnant and it was horrible. The not knowing and the not understanding why. But I didn't know what I was getting, so my dreams had an imaginary baby in them. Yours had a real-life vision of what they would be like. I am not comparing my loss to yours, but I can't imagine losing a baby when you had a clear idea of what they would look like.

**Evelyn:** **Oh Lucy, why didn't you say anything? You knew I'd had two losses previously. I would have understood.**

Lucy: I didn't want to put on to you. You were dealing with your own grief and I didn't want to put any pressure on you. Besides, it's not the done thing to talk about it, is it?

**Evelyn:** **Not if today is anything to go by.**

Lucy: Are you talking about lunchtime? If so, try and ignore them. You know, I think they mean well, it's just that they don't know the right things to say.

**Evelyn:** **You're probably right. It's just it still hurts, you know? And no, it's not just lunchtime. I lied when I said my day had been the same as yours. No-one sat me down and welcomed me back to work. I was just left to get on with things. I didn't even have a phone call last week to ask if there was anything I needed or wanted. I just feel invisible.**

Lucy: I wish I was invisible sometimes…

**Evelyn:** **Really?**

Lucy: Yeah, so I could be just Lucy, you know? Not Lucy whose mam has died… I feel guilty for all of the support I've had.

**Evelyn:** **Don't. It's just that your grief is acceptable and mine isn't. I have two kids at home to be thankful for. I don't need**

**to grieve.**

Lucy:        Don't be daft. You know that's not true.

**Evelyn:        I know. It's just hard when that's other people's opinions.**
**(*Pause.*) I suppose we should head back. People might start**
**wondering where we are. Well, you at least.**
**I'm invisible, remember?**

Lucy:        Well, you could pass by IT and give John's bum a pat!

**Evelyn:        Eh?**

Lucy:        Well, you are invisible, after all. Come on. And it might help
             to have a chat with Olivia. You never know.

**Evelyn:        Or I might get more bloody sense out of that brick wall!**

*Both head back to their desks.*

## Scene Six
*Evelyn and Lucy walk in. Manager and Colleague are at tea area.*

Manager:     Hey, where have you two been? We thought you had gotten lost?

Lucy:        Just having a quick catch up. Everything's ok now, though.
             Although I think Evelyn might want a chat.

**Evelyn:        No, no, I am fine. I'd rather just crack on, honestly.**

Lucy:        (*to Evelyn*) I'm sorry, but you're not getting away with this that
             easily. (*To Manager*) Evelyn needs a quick five-minute chat, that's
             all. I'm going to head back to my desk and give you two
             some space.

Colleague:   I'll come with you Lucy.

*Lucy and Colleague leave.*

Manager:     So, what's this about, Evelyn?

| | |
|---|---|
| **Evelyn:** | **It's nothing.** |
| Manager: | It's hardly nothing if Lucy has asked us to have a chat. |
| **Evelyn:** | **It's difficult.** |
| Manager: | I'm not that I'm unapproachable, am I? |
| **Evelyn:** | **It's about today.** |
| Manager: | Yes, and… |
| **Evelyn:** | **Well… You haven't exactly made me feel very welcome coming back. I feel like I have been ignored and left to get on with things. We didn't even have a return to work chat this morning.** |
| Manager: | Well, that's because I didn't think you would want to talk about it. And Sarah said that you wouldn't want to talk. I asked her what she wanted when she came back from something similar, and that's what she said. |
| **Evelyn:** | **You see, that's the problem. You didn't think. And I'm not Sarah. I needed a phone call or a chat to see what help or support I needed. Not a duplicate of what Sarah needed. And I told you last time this happened I needed a sit-down chat when I came back, just to feel supported.** |
| Manager: | Yes, well, most people don't want to talk about these things and just want to jump straight back in. I would probably do the same if there was a next time. |
| **Evelyn:** | **But who decides what most people want? I am telling you what I want and what I need, and you're dismissing me again.** |
| Manager: | I'm not. I'm just saying that I think that I did the right thing. |
| **Evelyn:** | **And I'm saying that you didn't. Not by me. Look, I don't want to go over this again. I just think that instead of guessing what people want or need that you should talk to them and then you'd know. Otherwise, you run the risk of them feeling** |

left out. That's all I'm saying. I don't want to argue about this anymore. I'm going to finish checking my emails and then head home. I am on an early finish today.

*Evelyn heads back to her desk, and Manager looks bemused before exiting the stage.*

*Music to indicate passing of the day and acting out work.*

**Evelyn:** *(looking at her phone)* **Three o'clock, and time to head home. Thank God today is over.**

Lucy: Are you leaving early today, too?

**Evelyn:** **Yeah, I don't think I could face another minute here.**

Lucy: So, your chat went well, then?

**Evelyn:** **Oh yeah, really well. She was adamant that she did the right thing in not talking to me, because Sarah in Sales said that that was what worked for her. I tried to tell her I wasn't Sarah in Sales, but she wasn't listening.**

Lucy: That's terrible.

**Evelyn:** **I know. I also said she shouldn't assume what people would want and she should have a conversation with the person, but that wasn't happening either. I think it's just because she doesn't know what to say. But she shouldn't make me feel bad for that.**

Lucy: No, she shouldn't. Look, I have to go, but you've got my number. Call me anytime, I mean it.

**Evelyn:** **You, too. And thanks for today. You have made a hard day more bearable.** *(They hug.)* **See you in the morning.**

*They both go off through different exits and curtains close.*

**Scene Seven**
*Curtains close during the sound effect below*

*Radio sound effect again*

So, we pick up where we left off yesterday, still on our topic of grief. Evelyn has been in touch to say she agrees with what has been said, and sadly her experience of returning to work today was met with mixed reactions. She has a poem which she would like to share, which will hopefully help someone out there know what to say in the future. She calls it 'Simply Say'. Over to you Evelyn:

I don't need to hear your stories
Of how friends did this or that
I don't need to hear it will be ok
And for you to give my arm a pat

I don't need to be told not to worry
And that will make things worse
Because I don't want to snap at you
And become sarcastic and terse

And when I tell you what's happened
And you don't know what to say
Don't tell me that I can try again
As there's always another day

And if I have children already
Please don't remind me of this
Because you're effectively saying
My lost baby, I shouldn't miss

Don't tell me it happened for a reason
Or at least it was early on
Because it doesn't change the fact
That my baby, they have gone

And don't tell me that I'll be over it
Because I will never forget
And I will always be sorry
That I'll have children I've never met

So, if you're looking for something to say
Words to show you care
Then please just say you're sorry
And that you will be there

Maybe an ear to listen
Or a shoulder on which I can cry
But please don't utter platitudes
Or try to explain to me why

I'm sorry is all it takes
There doesn't need to be anything more
I'm sorry is all I need
It's all I'm asking for

*Sound effect trails off - Lights down to indicate it's the end.*

# Dads Lose Babies Too – The Play

*Construction site. Ethan is sitting up against a half-demolished wall with his bait box. Owen enters.*

Owen:　　　　That wall really took a pummelling.

**Ethan:**　　　**What?**

Owen:　　　　You know, the one you practically took apart yourself.

**Ethan:**　　　Oh, aye, that one.

*They sit in silence, eating.*

Owen:　　　　Have you seen the new Avengers?
　　　　　　　It's meant to be really good.

**Ethan:**　　　**No.  Not yet.**

*More silence.*

Owen:　　　　Look, mate, are you alright?
　　　　　　　It's like pulling teeth, here.

**Ethan:**　　　**Well, I never did like the dentist.**

Owen:　　　　Seriously?!  Is that the best you have?

**Ethan:**　　　**It's the best you're gonna get.**

Owen:　　　　Are you gonna tell me what's up, or what?

**Ethan:**　　　**It's nothing.**

Owen:　　　　Bullocks. Can't be nothing.
　　　　　　　You've not said a word all day.

*More silence.*

**Ethan:**　　　**Abigail lost the baby.**

Owen:　　　　Oh, I'm so sorry, mate. I didn't know.

**Ethan:**   **It's alright.**

Owen:   So how is she?  She doing okay?
Sorry, that's a stupid question.  Listen.
If there's anything she needs, just you let me know.

**Ethan:**   **Will do.**

Owen:   So, how long have you two been trying?

**Ethan:**   **We hadn't actually decided.
It sort of just happened.
I was bricking it, to tell you the true,
but at the same time…**

**We had the first scan just the other week.  Couldn't make head nor tail of it myself.  Apart from the heart.  This little flutter you see in the middle.  Never felt anything like it.  Hits you like a train, a well of pride I've never felt before in my life, and before I knew it I was thinking about all the things I'd do as dad.  Taking her to her first day at school.  Show her all the classics I used to watch as a kid. Teach her to ride a bike.  All the little things.  I pictured her as a girl.  Isn't that odd?  Gone now.**

Owen:   I can't imagine what she's going through.
Do many other people know?

**Ethan:**   **Her sister knows.  And her friends have been great.
They've all been great.  There for her.
It's been hard.**

Owen:   Good.  It's good to know she's not alone.
I expect that helps.  Look, I've got to get back.
Patrick will kick off if I don't finish clearing up.
If I don't see you later, tell Abi I'm thinking
about her, will you?

**Ethan:**   **Will do.  Thanks, mate.**

Owen:   No problem.  See ya.

*Owen exits.*

*Recording:*

It's not just a mother's loss
The day a baby dies
It's not just the mother's ears
That will never hear their baby's cries

It's not one heart that breaks in two
And whose eyes shed many tears
It's not one set of hopes and dreams
That have been replaced with fears

A father's heart is broken, too
But he will keep this hidden
As for him to show his pain
Is something that feels forbidden

He might not break down and cry
He might be holding it together
But he too has lost a child
And that will stay with him forever

And maybe he feels torn
And doesn't quite know what to do
No doubt those who ask him how he is
Are far between and few
There may be guilt it wasn't him
That had to bear this pain
And all he could do was sit and watch
And his protection was in vain

And all this makes him lonely
And feel like there is nothing he can do
And although he didn't carry the baby
Dads lose babies too

*Ethan stands up and Owen enters.*

Owen:          Mate, listen, I've been a complete idiot.

**Ethan:**          **What do you mean?**

Owen:           Well, you. How are you?

**Ethan:**          **Eh? I'm… I'm…**
                        **(Looks down at his bait box.**
                        **Takes a breath as if trying to keep it together.)**

**Ethan:**          **I'm doing okay. Thank you for asking. I mean it.**

Owen:           Listen, I've been having a talk with the lads and we were thinking of going for a quick one before heading home. We wondered if you'd come long.

**Ethan:**          **Thanks, but I'm not sure.**

Owen:           Well, the offer's there, mate.

**Ethan:**          **Thanks. Appreciate it.**

Owen:           No problem. Listen, I'm not sure I'm the right guy for this, but if you ever just want to talk, or just meet up for a drink, let me know.

**Ethan:**          **Will do, thanks, mate.**

*Owen goes to leave, looking a little awkward and helpless
as to what he can do.*

**Ethan:**          **Owen?**

Owen:           Yeah?

**Ethan:**          **What time are you and the guys meeting?**

Owen:           Half five at the Rose and Crown. Oh, and the last one there buys the first round.

**Ethan:**          **Right.**

*Owen exits. Ethan puts away his bait box, picks up his equipment and exits.*

*The End.*

## About the Author

Angela is a poet, writer, playwright and actor.
She volunteers at 4Louis charity.

Angela has been writing as a way of coping with
complex emotions since she was a teenager.
She has used this coping mechanisms during her
journey though pregnancy and loss as a way of
helping herself and others.

The play, 'Simply Say' won an adjudicator's award at a
drama festival for the message that she was delivering.

This is her first published poetry collection.

Angela lives in the North East of England with
her husband and two daughters.

She can be found on Instagram under the handle
@angela_writes_life_and_loss.

# Where to go for help

If you feel like you need further support with your loss, whatever the stage of your journey, please see this list of organisations who can help:

**4Louis**
4Louis is a charity that works across the UK to support anyone affected by miscarriage, stillbirth and the death of a baby or a child.
**www.4louis.co.uk/**

**Miscarriage Association**
The Miscarriage Association is here to help anyone affected my miscarriage, molar pregnancy or ectopic pregnancy.
**www.miscarriageassociation.org.uk/**

**Aching Arms**
The charity Aching Arms is here to support and help you if you have suffered the loss of a baby during pregnancy, at birth or soon after.
**www.achingarms.co.uk/**

**Cradle**
Cradle charity provide a range of services to support anyone affected by early pregnancy loss.
**www.cradlecharity.org/**

**Tommys**
Tommys are the largest charity in the UK carrying out research into the causes of miscarriage, stillbirth and premature birth.
**www.tommys.org/**

**The Marisopa Trust**
The Marisopa Trust is a leading support charity primarily working within the field of baby loss and bereavement.
**www.mariposatrust.org/**

Illustration by Stacey Williamson-Michie @awesomemamaillustration

**Ectopic Pregnancy Trust**
The Ectopic Pregnancy Trust focuses on early pregnancy loss through ectopic pregnancy. They are the only charity in the world focusing on ectopic pregnancy, providing extensive general information and peer support for anyone experiencing the condition.
**www.ectopic.org.uk/about-us/**

**Sands**
Sands work to support anyone affected by the death of a baby; improve the care bereaved parents receive; and create a world where fewer babies die.
**www.sands.org.uk/**

Printed in Great Britain
by Amazon

86402983R00079